ABBA: Life After Forgiveness

Author: Danielle E. Edwards

Editor: Christopher Blueitt Jr.

Table of Contents

Introduction

This book is a short version of my life experiences, and situations where I had to find Forgiveness. Forgiveness was essential for me to be able to function and to keep my right mind. Hopefully, this book will bring an understanding that as human beings we all make decisions that affect the people in our lives. Somethings are out of our control sometimes but how we respond to them can be the making or breaking of us. No one wants to be stuck. Choose to Forgive. There is "Life After Forgiveness"

Preface

After losing my mother in 2012, it was pressed upon my heart to imagine how she felt leaving here before her time. We are told that our lives flash before our eyes when the time has come. The mind reflects back on the good and the bad. Even down to the decisions we make as parents, and how it affects our children's lives. I have found that it is how we deal with life's journey, and the energy we give back that allows us to complete the greatest task for us all. Taking care of a LIFE. Unforgiveness, can cause you to miss the big picture. Yet, I believe Forgiveness is "ABBA" GOD's way of restoring us back to Love. GOD IS LOVE.

Forward

ABBA means GOD as Father. In other languages this word is used to address a natural father. In this book I am using this term for both. There were times when I cried out to GOD - ABBA for direction, for his presence, as well as to soothe my pain. My natural father -ABBA, Kevin M. Brown whose presence has been consistent and adored, showed me how to develop an intimate relationship with GOD. So that my spirit can win in times where life was just so hard to get through. So it seemed. Just as GOD created us with the choice to believe or not to believe, and the possibility to be forgiven. There are times in life we have to forgive ourselves and others to move forward beyond our circumstances. Forgiveness to me is ABBA'S LOVE for us to experience and to share. GOD IS LOVE.

Chapter 1 The Call

Gasping for air, I never thought I'd leave here this way. The pain was nothing compared to knowing who and what I was leaving behind. My only seed. A daughter with my four beautiful grandchildren, who were probably calling me right now. Paralyzed as the tears ran down one side of my face. I would no longer be able to be there for her. This is the time I knew I needed to be there for her, more now than ever. I was supposed to be on the way the next day. I had already purchased my bus ticket and my bags were packed. I had caught the bus there a few times before. The ride was always short and simple. It was nice to see land and the open space full of agriculture.

As my breath got shorter, all I could think is no not right now, why now? I just started to pray as I could feel the foam rising up. Lord God forgive me of my sins, and help my daughter to forgive me too. Allow her to be everything you've created my only child to be. Please let her know I love her, I always have and I always will. My assignment has changed now, bring her through this surgery so she can continue to be the best mother she can be to my grandchildren, Amen.

As I took my last breath, I had peace. I knew that she would be okay. All the things in life she feared would now be over. As there were a lot of issues that were brought upon my daughter at an early age. Really too much for any child to endure. Things that she would carry for years, because of the decisions I made as a mother. Knowing that it's hard to forgive yourself for making bad or unhealthy decisions. Decisions that could alter your child's life and ultimately affect the decisions he or she makes.

At this very moment all I can say is I wish I would have listened to the warning of my mother. My child was my gift of unconditional love, to teach and to help grow.

How long would I have to lay here. Three days have gone by and the phone is still ringing, I know it's her calling me to see if I was still coming. This was the hardest thing I've ever had to go through. Can you imagine your child continuously calling for you and you can't answer. I wanted to so badly, frozen in time, never to speak, or laugh again. I'm sure I'm going to miss life. I thought I had secured a better future for myself and my family.

My mom's missing again girl, she said as she styled her friend's hair. I'm not going to think the worst were her thoughts. Her friend asked her if there was anything wrong, "I don't know, " was her reply, but in her heart she knew something wasn't right. A few minutes went by and she decided to call back home. Number after number nobody answered the phones. She called several times and left messages. Finally she got a hold of my baby brother," Uncle Corn have you heard from my mom? She's not answering the phone. She is supposed to be getting on the bus tomorrow, to help me after my surgery. He said he would give her a call, and go by there. Two more hours passed by and he never called back. So she left another voicemail, please call me back asap. By this time he had come by the house and saw the mail had piled up. Of course he knocked and called as many times as she did. Being an ex-firefighter that alarmed him to call 911. He called the situation in, and advised who he was, the squad came quick. One of the firefighters got off the truck and went straight to the window, which happened to be the only way to get in.

They had found half of me in the tub, and the other half face hovered over the toilet. It was kind of a relief to finally be acknowledged. Man but all I could think of was who would tell my daughter. She was miles away. How would she take the news, who would be there to console her?

As I was taken out of my home in a hazard bag, I thought about all the things I had created I had to leave behind. Tons of books, a plethora of journals, I wrote down just about my every thought. Glass stained lamp shades I satutored myself, umm I even taught myself how to play the keyboard. I had a great love of the arts and this brain of mine always stormed of ideas and solutions to whatever was going on in the world.

Hopefully one day people would understand who I really was, and that my life would be celebrated.

A well rounded African American woman that was gifted in so many ways and so was my daughter. As the day went on, she got a call from her father, he was stopping by, which was the norm. Out the blue he'd come and check on her and our grandkids. Hi Papa, how are you today, I'm good baby how are you? Do me a favor, he said to the oldest, you and your siblings go to your room, as they gave hugs and kisses as usual. I need to talk to your mother.

Dannie, you might want to sit down, her world stops when he calls her Dannie. That always let her know that something was serious. In the back of her mind she knew this conversation was going to be about me. They found your mom in her bathroom. Immediately she fell to her knees screaming no Daddy please don't tell me that. Why, why? Her anger raged far above the pain, Why my mom she didn't do anything to nobody! He grabbed her and embraced his daughter. No words, just a time when there's really nothing you can say. The kids came out of their rooms asking what was wrong? They all began to cry and were trying to make sure their mother was going to be okay. I believe if this happened two years ago she might have crawled into a hole and never come out. This wasn't the first time I left her.

Chapter 2 The Fall

1983 MJ was blowing up the pop charts, and the care bears decorated her room. I was attending the University of Toledo, majoring in Criminal Justice, and working part time at Taco Bell. I had taught her how to come home from school and how to lock the doors behind her. She would always do as she was told for the most part. After her afternoon snack she'd sit down and complete her homework if she had been assigned any. My daughter was a bright and loving child. I never had to worry about her not listening to my instructions. Things were quite rough at the time. As most mothers did back then we tried to keep our children from feeling the struggle. We had a conference coming up and I was saving what I could so we could attend in Chicago. Around this time the electricity was off, I came in that day and I found her sound asleep in the recliner chair lined with a blanket I crochet next to the window. I can only imagine her sitting there watching the sun go down and praying that she would see her dad's big orange pick up truck roll down the street. I knew she was a daddy's girl from the start because I was. I showed her how to catch the number five bus to her grandmothers, she had lived in the same place for years. Some days when I was scheduled to close I would tell her to go to your grandmothers after school. She loved that because she knew she would see her father there as well. I know what you're thinking at five years old. Why would I do that? That was dangerous, and anything could have happened. I just believed my child could handle it, it was a straight shot. Plus we were always catching the bus everywhere. I told her to always sit directly behind the bus driver, or by the front door. She never missed her stop. On those days I would call to confirm that she had made it there safely. Praise God she always did.

The ride to Chicago with the Baileys flew by, we were there in no time. It was exciting to see her head looking out of the windows at the windmills and the open land full of cows, and some horses. Nature excited the both of us. Fortunately I had a sister that showed her the world of agriculture by attending the

13

state fair every summer. Growing tomatoes and dandelions, riding the rides and eating cotton candy was a treat. Summer camp was fun too. We both got a little break, and enjoyed every moment.

We arrived on Friday night, class was packed and believe it or not, she would sing along to every song. She would even sneak her way to the front of the choir as if we didn't see her. Music made her happy, and she loved to dance. Saturday night I asked B to keep an eye on her. By that time the majority of the class members would be there. In other words it was party time. I didn't believe in letting my child see everything I did as an adult. I tucked her in the hotel bed and kissed her on the forehead good night. I rarely told her I loved her, not because I didn't, I know she already knew that. Well that night I wish I would have had. I didn't know I was going to return to the room changed forever. Alcohol was not my favorite thing to do, but I drank that night, heck I was among friends and class members. No harm, I just decided I had worked hard to make it on this trip, let me enjoy myself. I followed him to the room and sat for a minute to talk.

All of a sudden I wasn't feeling too hot, the room started spinning, and the weirdest feeling fell upon me. My mind raced back to the last drink I had downstairs. Nah, I had left my drink with my father to go to the restroom. Something ain't right. I slumped over. You can imagine the rest.

Danielle had woken up to multiple voices asking where I was. Someone spoke up and said" the last time I saw her she was with her father".

When I came to, the room was empty and I found myself having to put my clothes back on. I knew something happened, but I don't remember anything. Somehow I made it back to the room. My friends attended to me. They were quite angry asking me where I had been, and what happened. I didn't say anything. I just wanted to lay down and hold my baby. I made it back physically to her but the spirit I once had was gone.

15

The next morning was rough. I didnt attend class. I packed our bags and took my daughter to breakfast. I counted my money, it was all there. I couldn't bring myself to think that the man who created me, could or would do that to me. My mind was everywhere, these emotions overwhelmed me, I was ready to go. The more I thought about it the more angry I became. I coached her to take a nap, so I didn't have to talk.

We decided to stop at a Kmart, on the way home. I told my daughter to look at the clothes, I had more than enough money left over. She just kept walking away from me while I was trying to hold the clothes up to her. that made me snap. I hauled off and slapped her in her face. I remember the look in her eyes, we were both surprised. I had never put my hands on my daughter in that manner.

What I had just done to her, hurt me so bad I couldn't even say I'm sorry. Everyone saw and heard what I had done, and all I could do was just walk away.

That was the moment I realized something was truly wrong.

I'm sorry baby something is wrong with Mommy and I don't know what it is, she whispered in her ear. Bailey embraced her and walked her to the car. As soon as she got in, she said ``I'm sorry mommy I didn't listen, I'd just rather you get the electricity back on". Crushed me, my child was thinking about the conditions she knew she was going back to. So beyond her years, she knew I made a sacrifice to make this trip. Maybe my child had really been here before. She clinched to the back door, as we rode the whole way home in silence. That is when our relationship changed. It felt like we were strangers to one another, from that day forward. The silence between the two of us was piercing, and my soul was slowly dying. I lost my mind and my daughter at the same time. My mother warned me to stay away from him. He tried to do the same mess to two of my eldest sisters. My mom, his wife threatened his life, but that didn't stop him. For some reason my daughter had always been able to see that

17

devious spirit in him. She would say I don't feel confedo, she couldn't say comfortable. In one night my life had changed. What happened to me would affect the life of my daughter as well. We just grew further and farther apart.

Chapter 3 The Visit

We were visiting my sister and my father popped up to her apartment. Danielle immediately started to act out. My sister asked her what's wrong with you? Recognizing her whole demeanor changed. 'I don't like him. My sister looked in disbelief as Danielle stared at him with anger in her eyes. Okay baby, lets go get some snacks at the drive thru. The drive thru was located directly across the parking lot. There was quite a wait though. As they entered back into the apartment, there I was again spaced out laying on the couch, he was standing at the bathroom sink zipping up his pants, then washed his hands. What the hell is going on? my sister asked. He looked at her and then he looked at me and left.

He had the nerve to show up at my apartment a few days later, asking me for the notes from the last Bible class. I ushered Danielle to her room, you stay in here and don't come out. I closed the door behind me and I began to question him about what he had done to me. Of course he told me I was crazy, and at the same time he said If I had it my way I'd have all yall on the streets. Okay it's time for you to go. Your mind, if you think I will ever agree to that. You got to go, scaring my baby. I know she heard us yelling. After he left I peeked in her room to check on her. She wasn't in her bed, I called out for her, and she came from out the closet. I picked her up and told her, I won't ever let anything happen to you. Is he gone? she asked as she pulled the covers over her head. I was losing it on the inside, I couldn't tell anyone what had happened to me, I was his daughter, a full grown adult. It hurt me to the point I just stayed in denial, the more I denied what he had done to me, the harder things got for me.

I decided to pack some bags and go over my moms for a couple days. Just in case he was still in the city. I couldn't have my daughter afraid to be in her house. I knew my mother wasn't having any mess. He wasn't allowed to step on her porch, let alone come into her house. She had left him a long time ago. Being from Puducah, Kentucky my mom stayed strapped. Pearl in her purse and a rifle in the trunk of her Cutlass. She was licensed to carry and didn't care who you were. She would sure nough give it to you if you were asking for it. Granmaw he came by the house a couple times Danielle told her. He did something to my mommy, I don't like him. My mom knew what he was capable of and she believed my daughter. She never confronted me about it, but she sure did say didn't I tell you to stay away from him, over and over again.

Chapter 4 The Fire

This had become too much for me to take mentally, I needed help with my daughter, so I decided to stay a little longer over to the house. A couple days later I got a phone call saying that the apartment had caught on fire. The fire started downstairs and spread to the second floor where we stayed. We lost everything, after that I was done. It just seemed like all that I worked hard for was being stripped away from me. I was a strong woman, highly intelligent, but maybe I was just too trusting. Our landlord sat the apartment on fire for insurance money. How can a person be so selfish as if our things, our home did not hold any value.

I found myself back in the sticks at my mother's house permanently. This house was actually moved to its location, and it was the biggest house on the block. This house stayed full of people all the time. I had eight siblings, and we had fun growing up. My mother was a nurse, and worked hard to care for us all in spite of his absence. I guess being from the south made you a little stronger when you needed to be. Mom was humble, but don't get it twisted. She carried a gun in her purse and a rifle in the trunk of her car, could cuss like a sailor and meant every word. On the sweeter side she baked breads and pies from scratch, and told the best stories ever. Gwen was definitely cut from a different cloth. She endured a lot while taking care of us and her grandchildren. I am grateful for her to have had her as a mother.

Did you take my cigarettes little girl? as I found myself snatching my daughter up again. No ma'am, I did not! I'm only seven years old. I don't even like the smell of them. I actually argued with her and told her yes you did, I know you did. I made her go in the sun room for hours. I guess I forgot she was in there. Where is Danielle? my sister asked me, I told her she was asleep. Well did she eat? she asked. I walked away and got ready for work. Come on out of there, you've been in there long enough. I never really thought about my actions and how they could possibly make her feel. I was a ticking time bomb on the inside and really didn't

23

care. nobody seemed to care about mine. I was always blaming my daughter for everything, so much that day I decided to burn her arms with a cigarette, and that was the last straw for my mother. She came home from work and found Danielle hiding in the corner of the sunroom crying and praying to God for me. She showed her what I had done and was waiting for me on the porch when I got back to the house. The next thing I know, I was riding to the state hospital for the first time. I knew this hurt my mother more than it hurt me, but It needed to be done. I had lost it, and I didnt know how to deal with the fact my own father micked me and sexaully abused me. How could a father do that to his own daughter? Now I wasn't able to take care of my precious gift any more. Mom stepped up to the plate, and made sure Danielle was taken care of. To be honest all of the family did. I hadn't seen her in months. The meds they put me on calmed me but I hate being confined. I was always a free spirited person, so to be strapped to a bed like I was possessed by the devil was truly an awakening for me. What happened to me consumed my every thought and scarred my heart. I was no longer myself, and my past took over the present and my future. I had stayed in denial for too long, with no one to talk to but these four walls.

The holidays rolled around and my family decided to bring her to visit me. It was hard for me to let my daughter see me like this. I was ashamed, embraced and hurting. I felt like she hated me, like I failed her as a mother. I did know how to show her my love for her anymore. So I keep my distance. I'm pretty sure she wanted to hug and love on me, but how could she. She was probably afraid that I would reject her. I had abused her, both mentally and physically. We both missed the feeling you have between a mother and a daughter, especially when you hugged. Unconditional love is hard to come by. But when it's been broken it's even harder to heal. I had done the same thing to her as he had done to me. Now I was locked in a place where the people had to be just as crazy to work there as the patients. This place was for people who didn't have it all. Although I'm here right now, what I have learned throughout my life could never be taken away from me.

25

Unfortunately she saw what happened, even though she was young she remembered what I was afraid to admit to anyone else. I know if I had told my mother she'd hunt him down like a dog. If I had told my brothers and sisters maybe it would change what they thought of our father. I didn't think that it was my responsibility to alter anyone's feeling of love or respect for their parents. God just made my true heart like that. I was ready to get back to living and utilizing every gift the creator had blessed with me. Seeing my daughter and hearing her voice gave me the inspiration but these meds altered what I showed to others. I had to face the reality alone that I was a beautiful woman that had been tainted by her father. Until then I felt hopeless at times, not worthy of seeing the sun rise the next morning. Simply gone with the wind. Some days I had the mental capacity to pray for her, I felt like that was all I could do. The older she got the more I decided to stay where I was mentally, see when you've planted a seed, a seed that can grow into bitterness and it's your fault, what can you do. Instead of making her feel security, this thing made her feel unwanted by the one who created

her. Only the love of God could penetrate what I knew
to be a generation curse now. I wasn't the only daughter
he had done this to. Yeah my father was a true work of
art. He was married only to my mother, but it's said that
he has twenty seven kids and counting. I was told back
in his hay days he was a con artist. Maybe that would
explain how he was able to ride around in a white
convertible Cadillac, dressed in all white with a dobb
on. Big belly and all looking like the colonel. He had
started a fire in my heart, as well as my daughters.
Hopefully she wouldn't have to live her life with the
same flames as I did. Self condemnation fueled the
flames. Praying one day she'd know how to put the fire
out for the both of us. Our hearts, our home and now
our relationship.

Chapter 5 The Lonely

Danielle was an only child if you hadn't figured that out by now. She was loved by her family, but nothing or no one could take the place of me, her mother. She looks like me, thought just the same as me. Very intelligent, strong willed and good with her hands. Completely creative in big and small ways. When she was born she had veils over her eyes. This is a slight film that actually would have to be pulled off. It's said babies that are born this way have the ability to see in the spirit realm. In other words she could see spirits, may they have been good or bad. I always felt that she was special and would make a difference in this world. I planned to finish my degree in criminal justice, and make sure that she had everything she needed to make it in her lifetime. I always explained to her my every move, so she would have the ability to use her common sense to make good decisions. Sometimes having the need to achieve great things kept you on the path to succeed. On the contrary, this made her overthink everything. It muffled her voice as a child, and I made

her more inquisitive about everything. Being
motherless, she had to grow up faster than other
children whose mother was in their life. She gravitated
to the people around her in my absence. And it seemed
like she was going to be fine. She had a village but still
seemed to be alone. No one to get in trouble with, no
one to share the secrets of her heart. No one listened to
the things that bothered her the most. Sometimes I wish
she would have asked me about the things that she had
seen me go through. I never brought it up to her,
because I didn't want her to remember it let alone be
torned. Maybe God chose her to be the one to break the
generational curse, and I didnt want to put my hands on
it. I don't know if this was the best decision for her, but
I know she had a father in heaven that would help her.
All she needed to do was to keep on believing in love,
protect herself, and preserve her body. One day she'd be
able to love and be loved in the manner God had
created man and woman to experience. Not the images
she had seen, nor the noises or voices she had heard.
Instead this little girl amazed me with the joy in her
voice when we talked on the phone. She would tell me

29

how much she missed me and that she couldn't wait to see me again. Somehow she remembered my smile and the way that I would look at her. She longed for my hugs and fried eggs on rye bread. My daughter never stopped loving me, or loving others no matter how much pain she was in. Not every child is able to fight through abandonment. This little girl did, what happened didn't make her bitter like it made me. She decided to love better and harder. I say this because, while I was in this institution, I'd receive cards and drawings from her in the mail. Talking about how we used to ride the bus to the zoo. Chase butterflies in the park, and how we'd go get ice cream on hot days. Innocent she was in this life of mine. We were both lonely but we didn't give up!

Chapter 6 The Change

It has been over a year now that my mother has taken care of her. Between the third shift and being tired, she spent most of her time alone. Lost in her own thoughts. Even though she knew she was loved. It sure didn't feel like it. I'm not saying all her days were bad ones, but it sure needed to change for her.

Standing in the hallway of the court house, My mother told her father I'm not going to fight you for custody. You have always provided for your daughter. Danielle needs to be with one of you. Danielle looked at my mother with tears in her eyes but her heart rejoiced at the same time. She felt like she was being passed around, yet she loved her daddy just as much as she loved me. I'm glad that my mother decided that it would be in the best interest for my daughter to be with her Daddy. I had been abandoned, and I didnt want my daughter to feel the same way as I do. Her father was a good man. Hard working and believed in God as well. Although we did not work out, we made someone beautiful. A soul that was worth fighting and sacrificing for. She was in good hands and I knew that even though I didn't want things to go this way. I was supposed to be there for her, but there were some things standing in the way.

The conversation that hurt her the most is when I told her " I didn't have any children by Kevin Brown". She was nine years old hearing her own mother telling her basically you're not my child. She screeched out the pain of hearing those words. As she slammed the phone down her blood began to boil and her nose started to bleed immediately. It felt like someone had been pounded on her head and tied her upside down to a ringing church bell. This was the darkest moment she had encountered. Her body felt her heart bled for the both of us. Her grandmother came rushing down the stairs. Danielle, please tell me what happened? She was in such shock she could barely get the words out. My mother told me I wasn't hers. She said she didn't have any children by no Kevin Brown. Baby she didn't mean to say that. Sit back, we have to get your nose to stop bleeding. Her nose bled for almost an half an hour, she balled herself on the couch with an ice pack to her nose and a cold towel on her head. What I said she had internalized. I made her become the angry little girl I was feeling like on the inside. Saying something like that to a child would completely confuse them, but I wasn't in my right mind as her grandmother told her. Unfortunately she was right. I was never the same. Anger became her secret friend , she lost her smile and the hope of me coming back to get her one day. I would live with guilt up until my dying day. All I have now was these four walls and these meds that seem not to be working. Who in the hell were these people to have me locked up here like I was a wild animal to be mastered. Hiding behind a piece of paper, as if they knew me or what I had been through. Hell I just lost my daughter and no one seems to care.

It felt just like me lying in that tub and feeling the life leaving my body. Instead I was still breathing. Existing but dying on the inside was my reality for years. Losing unconditional love, will have you sitting back and wishing you had the power to turn the hands of time. When you realize the damage you've caused your child, your purpose changes. It can take you to another level of being a human being in such a cruel world.

As parents when we hurt we should be making conscious decisions that would protect our children. We are human and will make mistakes. I was warned and I didnt listen. As the years went by all I could do is pray that my daughter wouldn't carry the burden into her relationships that she'd have in her adulthood.

Chapter 7 The Eye

It was his eighth-grade graduation the first time she saw him. He was the valedictorian of the graduating class. Fair skinned with dark curly hair. As she listened to his words she began to smile, he was fine, were her thoughts. Soon as the ceremony was over, she ran to her sister and asked who he was. She wanted to congratulate him on his achievement. She searched the grounds for Charles Woods, but he had left the building.

Summer had passed, and it was November 16th of the following school year when she heard his name being announced for birthdays of the day. Wow he's here she said. Happy Birthday she said as she speed walked passed him standing at his locker. He turned around and told her thank you, he was smiling hard as he lifted his head to see her face. She kept walking thinking to herself. I don't care if he's younger than me. He's cute, smart and can dress. You're welcomed she yelled as she zoomed down the stairs. Sweaty palms and a racing heart is what happened every time she saw him. He never really said too much to her, and life went on. She graduated and went away to college.

During the winter break of her freshman year at K-State, she went up to the high school, as all alumni did. This time he made sure he said something to her first. He even asked for her number. Needless to say it was a good break. They went to the movies for their first date, and he paid for everything. Although he was young he had a little cash flow. He knew she was going back to school but he didnt care. It was time for her to go back to school but the weather was bad. She kept asking her dad if they could wait until Sunday to take her back to school. She just had a bad feeling about something. Plus she wanted to spend more time with Charles. Her father said no we cant wait I have to go back to work on monday. On the way down I 75 she was sleeping and all of a sudden she woke up to the ceiling of the van turning in a circle. He had hit a patch of black ice that sent the van into the guardrail, but the force flipped them down the embankment. Turned out it was actually illegal for them to be on the road. It seems like they were sitting there for hours. He had to punch out the front windshield to exit the van. He was gone for 15 mins but came back to warm up, no one would stop for him standing on the side of the road. He went back up again, he had to get help for us. Finally someone stopped and called 911. We had to be pulled up by sleds, and made the front page of the local newspaper the next day. It wasn't their time to go, but out of the mouth of babes. Her father ended up telling her I wish I would have listened to you, the van is gone but I'm glad we're all okay.

Danielle got a chance to spend time with Charles again as she wanted before returning back to school. They wrote to each other every week, he would sometimes send her greeting cards with a little something in it to help her. This made her forget about the age difference.

All she wanted was someone to treat her right and to be honest with her. She was excited to have him in her life. Charles was rushing home in a little Dodge Neon, someone had hit the Toyota Camry that Danielle

37

had always wanted. The tires hit a patch of black ice and catapulted the car into a tree. As he waited and waited for help all he could think of was his daughter and how he wished he would have just slowed down. He didnt know which pain was greater, the pain he was physically feeling or the pain of not knowing he would have the chance to live and be with his daughter. The car had lodged on the drivers side, and the impact caused brain damage. The swelling was so bad they had to cut into his skull to relieve some of the pressure. This happened three days before his daughter's birthday. Charles too had experienced losing his mother, although she was still alive she wasn't present in his life due to the usage of drugs. I believe this is what draws the two of them together. Months had gone by, as he fought to live with 70% percent brain damaged. They labeled him as a vegetable. He was twenty three years old when this happened. Spending his last days and nights in a nursing home. When Danielle would visit she would play a handheld recorder of Jordans voice, saying hi daddy I love you and I miss you, can't wait until you get better. Some days he would let the tears roll down his face. that would be his way of letting Danielle know that he could hear and how he was feeling. Love by Musiq Soul Child was Danielle's way of letting Charles know that she still loved him in spite of the past. She laid the recorder on his shoulder as she groomed his feet, and made sure he was properly covered. Open your mouth so I can clean it out. she would love on him as if there was nothing wrong with him at all. Sometimes they both cried for Jordan at the sametime. She didn't want Jordan to come every visit, it was so hurtful to see him like that with no change. She would even pray at his bedside and read the word of God to him. She wanted them to be a family, more than anything. Day after day, night after night, tears after tears she would be by his side. One thursday she came in with a new energy. She told him that she wanted to move to Columbus now, he had tried to get her to move there together. His job would have transferred him. But she was too scared. If you want to still be a family with me and Jordan, get up out of this bed right now. He lifted his arms and feet, he tried with all of his might. Her heart raced at his efforts, she was excited to see

39

him move like that. I wished we would have left when you asked me to. Sometimes you have to face your fears, it could possibly be your way of escape. It gave her hope as she knew she had a job interview on the following Monday in Columbus. She left the nursing home that night sharing what happened, hopeful that he was going to get better.

Danielle had tossed and turned all night. Monday morning came and she woke up to the earliest feelings. As she got ready for the interview, her sister came into the room with the phone in her hand. It's Auntie she needs to talk to you. Charles had passed away. She couldn't understand how that was even possible, she just saw him try to get out of that bed. Maybe he was just tired now. The accident happened in March and it's June now. She couldn't bring herself to tell their baby girl Jordan that her dad was gone. Both of her sisters explained to her that he was an angel now.

Danielle was numb, and had to take the bus back home to Toledo. It seemed as if the two hour ride was a five hour ride. The tears kept falling as she popped tylenol for her headache. The disbelief imbued her eyes as her heart played frames of her Boaz over and over. She thought about the first day she saw him, and how her baby girl didn't have her dad anymore.

It was the day before the funeral when she walked outside and her car was gone. Charles paid her car note, he'd always taken care of the both of them financially. She went back to the apartment to call for a ride so that she and Jordan would have something to wear to his funeral. This time in her life was hard being in school and having to keep it moving was rough. Fortunately she had a skill to keep the ends meet. Often she wouldn't eat to make sure her daughter was full. There were times she would say girl , I will do your hair, just make sure you cook enough for Jordan to eat. The weight dropped off her too fast, people thought she was sick. Really her heart was, and you could see it.

Black dress with matching periwinkle shoes and purse, the opposite for Jordan periwinkle dress with black patent leather shoes and purse. That's the best she could do at meijers. It didn't matter anyway. As long as

41

they were put together. Charles wouldn't have had it any other way. Saying goodbye to the apple of her eye was one of the hardiest things she ever had to endure. She went against all odds to be with him. At one point in time, you'd think she loved him more than she loved God by her actions.

Chapter 8 The Unexpected

Dannie I need you to go to VA with me to do this video shoot, says her cousin. Meechie was a go getter, very strong minded and beautiful inside and out. We had come from a background of strong women. They went to VA and accomplished what she had set out to do. It was a much needed trip and experience for Danielle. By this time Danielle was married with four children. She was a stay at home mom, and she had to set her goals and ambitions aside. So to be in her element and helping felt good, and was what she needed. Her cousin knew that about her. We can't lose ourselves in our daily responsibilities. You must take time for yourself. Honey this young lady, her cousin was truly fearless, and she would always find a way to make it happen. Plus she had a mouthpiece of a lawyer.

Hey lady, guess what. Danielle said what as she let her in the door. Meechie said I'm here to give you a break. I'm going to watch the kids you are going to take my car to, here's some money, go do something for yourself. You have until 10pm. What, Danielle replied"

girl I can't let you do that. you're out of your mind".
Long story short She wasn't taking no for an answer.
Danielle had her time and returned home to the kids in
bed and the kitchen was cleaned. Being at home with
two in pullups and one in diapers was no joke, for
Danielle. It is really her biggest challenge in life with
being an only child until her Dad had married.
Sometimes people that care will be exactly what you
need without even asking.

Meechie called Danielle from the hospital, she
had been there for the second time within seven days. It
was her third day there. " I need you to go get
something from my house. Danielle immediately made
arrangements for the kids, she left the shelter, dropped
the kids off and got to the hospital as fast as she could.
The sight of her cousin frightened her. She was sedative
and just not looking herself. Man why didn't you call
me before now, she asked her. You're going through
alot, I didn't want to bother you. I need some clothes,
undergarments etc. No problem Danielle replied. So
what is going on, what is the doctors saying? The

doctors had put the biopsy of her colon in the dye, and hadn't looked at it since Monday . Today was Wednesday, SMH. I think you need to go somewhere else, this hospital specializes in child birth not trauma.. I will, Meechie said, as soon as I get some strength. Okay well I will be back. As Danielle left the building she prayed all the way to her cousin's apartment that they would find out what was wrong , and that her cousin would go to a different hospital. She knew she came back to this particular one because it was the closest to her house. Her cousin was in alot of pain. You could see it in her face. That's not what all Danielle saw either, but she dared not say it.

She went to the apartment and grabbed her things. As she looked for the things she asked for, she noticed a lot of empty boxes of laxatives. She knew she had some issues but she ate right, didn't drink or smoke, and she had a consistent workout plan. Danielle hurried back to the hospital. This is everything you asked for, do you need anything else? No thanks though I appreciate you doing this for me. Danielle made sure

45

her cousin was comfortable, sat with her for a little while longer. The nurse came in to pass her more meds but no doctor. Danielle had to hold the cup to her cousin's mouth for her to drink the water. This blew her mind to see her that way. Her eyes welled with tears she dare not let fall. She kissed her and told her she loved her, and that she would call when she got back to the shelter to see what the doctor said. Meechie nodded her head to acknowledge what was said. Reluctantly, Danielle left and called her cousin's mother and told her that her child didn't look too good, and she believed that she should go to another hospital. Less than five hours later, she got a call, please go back to the hospital she crashed, and had to have an emergency surgery. In disbelief Danielle was the only person at the hospital waiting for the surgeon to come out. Her parents lived back home and were on their way. He came out and said that he had to remove a large amount of her colon. The whole left side of her colon was dead. And that she couldn't live without it. Basically if she makes it she'd have a bag. The news made Danielle gage, cry, and ask why at the same time. How could this happen, if the colon was dead they should have been able to tell when they took the biopsy, she said to the surgeon. Your probably right mamm, but this is not my hospital they called me in just for her.

This feeling was all too familiar for Danielle, but she was even more angry this time. Now she was angry with herself for not making her cousin get up and go to another hospital. Having to call her mom with this news seemed unfair on both ends, but she did and she waited for everyone to get there. It was the meds that made this situation worse. Morphine shot her liver and kidney that night. When this happens the body has to work harder than before to recover. Her parents were advised to get her to a hospital that deals with trauma and they made it happen. Meechie kept fighting, and there were times when we were happy with her progress.

Danielle was by her side as much as she could be, even until her last breath. She flatlined as he mother was talking to her and holding her hand as Danielle was holding her mother's hand.

47

Danielle Turned to the nurse and advised her that her mom doesn't know what just happened. Danielle was watching the monitor while everyone else was looking at her. The nurse grabbed her hands and told her she was gone. The scream will never leave her head as she watched her big cousin lose her daughter. The pain in her voice was something you'd wish you never heard.

Palms were sweating and her stomach turning as she played Halo over in her head. She danced at her first funeral. This song was perfect because she knew that her cousin was her Angel now.

Chapter 9 The Strong

Thank you for taking care of me when my Mother couldn't. I love you, see you soon. Were Danielle's last words to her grandmother, my mother. She turned and kissed her on the cheek, I believe she knew exactly who was talking to her. That trip home had been completed. it's hard to see all your family when you come to visit. Danielle got on the road that Sunday before Easter, feeling good about all the faces she was able to see and the time that was spent with family and friends. She was ready to spend the next day with her kids and enjoy Easter Sunday.

Four o'clock that morning the phone rang, I'm sorry baby Granmaws gone. Tears Imbued her face once again, but this time she was free from guilt. It almost seemed as if my mother had been waiting to hear those words from Danielle. Although she was hurt and sad over her transition she was grateful to the Holy Spirit for speaking to her to go by grandmaws before she left to go back home. The words she spoke to her grandmother was truly from her heart. Who wouldn't be thankful for someone doing the things that your mother should have done. Granmaw did more than just shelter and fed her. She taught her how to be strong and the importance of working hard and never giving up. Never complaining about her life but making the best out of any situation. She left her her wisdom and strength. She did her best to be there for her always and that meant more to her than anything. I believe she knew Danielle would need all that she had given.

Some years before my mother passed three generations came together and remodeled the house. New paint , new furniture, and a new found love and appreciation for all that she had done. Being in that ole house without that southern girl from Kentucky just wasn't the same. Losing her was hard on all of us. No matter what my mom always made sure you had a home to come back to. It's funny how sometimes we don't look at life differently until we lose them, and to have known someone who was good makes you see them in the light that God sees them.

Chapter 10 The One

A few days before new years Danielle decided that she wasn't going to let nothing stand in her way any more. That everything in her past would be exactly that, the past. The only thing she felt was holding her back was her unforgiveness she had toward my father and how his decision to do what he did to me affected her directly.

Buddy was standing in Danielle's kitchen when she revealed to him what my father had done to me in the past. This was the second time she had seen him that angry. He was so upset he responded to a mass text message addressed to the family. *#@% him don't ever send anything about that !#**@ to my phone again! She was in shock to see him respond like that. But to be honest we were both satisfied at the same time. You see I never chose to bad mouth my father, and although my mother listened to Danielle, she never spoke of his evil doing towards me, it wasn't a secret anymore.

Two days later Buddy called Danielle and told her that her grandfather had passed away. She rejoiced and praised God in that moment, not that she was happy that he died but the fact that she had forgiven him. He would have had power over her from the grave if she didn't allow the love of God to reside in her heart so that she might be able to forgive. Those couple days before the new year she declared her freedom and literally took her hands and pulled the stronghold of unforgiveness off her mind, body and soul.

By the time she made it to the funeral the last remarks were being given. She was sharp as a toothpick, the church was full and dry. Sitting in the back puels, where no one could really see her and she wanted it that way. She had cried all the tears she would ever cry because of him. It was God that she even decided to show up, but it was honorable that she did. The funeral wasn't the big moment Danielle thought it would be. She had already said goodbye to the physical and spiritual pain of the generational curse.

Chapter 11 ABBA Father

I have to be honest with you. If it wasn't for a father's love for his daughter, Danielle would have endured life's challenges alone. In this story her father was always there. Not perfect but present. That is how GOD is, always present. Every human being has a father in Heaven that loves his children. Though life may not always be fair, and just the existence of evil can try to keep you from believing in love. God is love, and God shows us how to love one another. Love kept me from dying in self-condemnation. Love kept my daughter through all the loss she experienced in life. Love is what allowed her to forgive in order to be the best person she can be in this world. Though it may have seemed to be her truth that she suffered a lot, and lacked the love I wanted to give her. God gave her a natural father that prayed and fought with her. He taught her how to fight against her worst fears. I thank God for love, love of oneself that ensures you to make it. Love of others that brings peace in the storms. Love that creates ways when it seems to be no way. Love that conquers all. Love breaks any curse we as humans experience. Love displayed when life was created. Love that corrects us when we fall. We have to allow love to imbue our hearts through all things, ignorance, injustice, hatred, poverty, sickness, and even in death. Forgiveness is the way to Love, know that there's *" Life After Forgiveness"*

Conclusion and Dedications

This book is dedicated to my: Angels

Vari L. Edwards

Charles L.Woods

Demetria S.Hibbler

Gwendolyn H. Edwards

I'm so grateful to have loved you all. Thank you for the lessons I've learned in my life because of loving you. Keep guiding me MY ANGELS!

Love always, Dannie aka. Danielle E'Lissa Edwards